WHAT IS A
MAMMAL?

Robert Snedden

Photographs by Oxford Scientific Films

Illustrated by Adrian Lascom

Sierra Club Books for Children
San Francisco

Text copyright © 1993 by Robert Snedden
Photographs copyright © 1993 by Oxford Scientific Films and individual copyright holders
Format and illustrations copyright © 1993 by Belitha Press Limited

First U.S. Edition 1994

First published in Great Britain in 1993 by Belitha Press Limited, 31 Newington Green, London N16 9PU

Library of Congress Cataloging-in-Publication Data

Snedden, Robert.
    What is a mammal?/Robert Snedden; photographs by Oxford Scientific Films; illustrated by Adrian Lascom.
        p.   cm.
    "First published in Great Britain in 1993 by Belitha Press Limited . . ."—T.p. verso.
    Includes index.
    ISBN 0-87156-468-8
    1. Mammals—Juvenile literature. [1. Mammals.] I. Lascom, Adrian, ill. II. Oxford Scientific Films. III. Title.
QL706.2.S64 1994
599—dc20   93-26145

Printed in Hong Kong for Imago
10 9 8 7 6 5 4 3 2 1

Editor: Rachel Cooke
Series designer: Frances McKay
Designer: Vivienne Gordon
Consultant: Dr. Jim Flegg
Educational consultant: Brenda Hart

The publisher wishes to thank the following for permission to reproduce copyrighted material:

Oxford Scientific Films and individual copyright holders on the following pages: Doug Allan, 18 bottom; Kathie Atkinson, 22; Ron Austing/Photo Researchers Inc., 27; Anthony Bannister, 10, 16; Eyal Bartov, 11 bottom right; Lloyd Beesley/Animals Animals, 13 bottom left; Nick Bergkessel/Photo Researchers Inc., 19 top; Aldo Brando Leon, 17 top left; Carolina Biological Supply Co., 13 bottom right; Martyn Colbeck, cover, 11 bottom left; Dr. J. A. L. Cooke, 5 top; Stephen Dalton, 25; Tim Davis/Photo Researchers Inc., 1; Dr. E. R. Degginger/Animals Animals, 11 top; Phil A. Dotson/Photo Researchers Inc., 4 top; Michael Fogden, 15 bottom right; Howard Hall, 28–29; Johnny Johnson/Animals Animals, 6 top; Hubert Kranemann/Okapia, 12 bottom; Dean Lee, 7; Zig Leszczynski/Animals Animals, 12 top; David Macdonald, 15 bottom left; S. G. Maglione/Photo Researchers Inc., 4 bottom; Stan Osolinski, 3; Richard Packwood, 14, 14–15, 23 bottom; Partridge Productions Ltd, 24; Robin Redfern, 23 top; Hans Reinhard/Okapia, 18 top; Philip Sharpe, 16–17; Wendy Shattil and Bob Rozinski, 26 top; Marty Stouffer Productions/Animals Animals, 8–9; Tony Tilford, 17 top right; Steve Turner, 5 bottom; Merlin D. Tuttle/Photo Researchers Inc., 19 bottom; Konrad Wothe, 6 bottom; Belinda Wright, 26 bottom.

Front cover picture: The cheetah is the fastest animal on land.

Title page picture: The jaguar is one of the larger members of the cat family.

Contents page picture: The gemsbok lives on the grasslands of southern Africa.

CONTENTS

WHAT IS A MAMMAL?

What do you think of when you think of a mammal? Perhaps this isn't a word you've heard before and you don't immediately think of anything at all. Every one of us sees some mammals every day. Many people keep mammals as pets. Cats and dogs are mammals, as are mice and hamsters. Many farm animals are mammals as well, including cattle, sheep and horses.

▲ The weasel is an alert hunter. This short-tailed weasel lives in the United States.

◀ Apes, such as this gibbon from Southeast Asia, are among the most intelligent of the mammals. Humans are a type of ape too.

◀ The wombat of Australia is a member of a group of mammals called marsupials (see page 13).

Mammals come in many shapes and sizes. Wombats and weasels are mammals; so are giraffes and gibbons. A whole range of animals are mammals. They may not look the same, but all of them have certain things in common — things that make them different from other animals. You will find out what those things are as you read this book.

If you want to see one of the commonest mammals, all you have to do is look in a mirror. You are a mammal too.

▶ The long neck of the giraffe allows it to eat parts of plants that other animals can't reach. This giraffe lives in Kenya in Africa.

FUR AND HAIR

Polar bears have thick fur coats that protect them from the cold and wet conditions of the Arctic.

One of the first things you notice about most of the mammals you see is that they have fur or hair. Think of a cat's fur or the hair on top of your head. Hair is made of a substance called **keratin** and grows from the skin. Mammals are the only animals that have a furry coat. All mammals have hair but some have very little. Whales, for instance, only have a few bristles.

A mammal's hair helps to keep it warm. Mammals that live where it is very cold often have great shaggy coats. Polar bears have such thick fur that even when they swim their skin stays dry. Every hair has a small muscle attached. These muscles can raise or lower the hairs to allow air to move through the hairs to adjust the animal's temperature. Sometimes when you are cold, goose bumps appear on your skin. This happens when the muscles pull on the hairs to trap air to make you warmer. You can find out more about the way mammals keep warm on pages 8 and 9.

▶ Some mammals, such as these fighting wolves, raise their fur to make themselves look bigger and stronger.

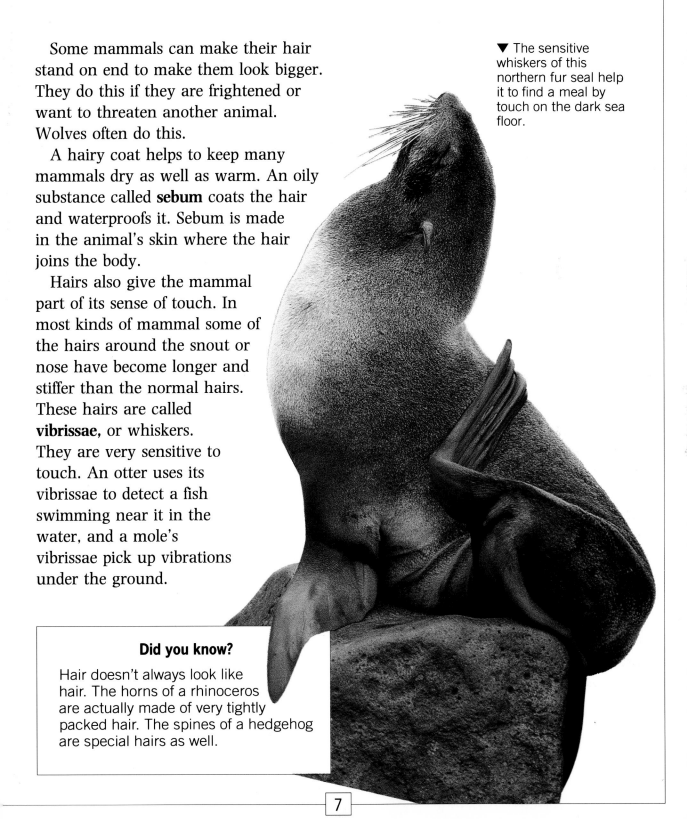

Some mammals can make their hair stand on end to make them look bigger. They do this if they are frightened or want to threaten another animal. Wolves often do this.

A hairy coat helps to keep many mammals dry as well as warm. An oily substance called **sebum** coats the hair and waterproofs it. Sebum is made in the animal's skin where the hair joins the body.

Hairs also give the mammal part of its sense of touch. In most kinds of mammal some of the hairs around the snout or nose have become longer and stiffer than the normal hairs. These hairs are called **vibrissae,** or whiskers. They are very sensitive to touch. An otter uses its vibrissae to detect a fish swimming near it in the water, and a mole's vibrissae pick up vibrations under the ground.

▼ The sensitive whiskers of this northern fur seal help it to find a meal by touch on the dark sea floor.

Did you know?

Hair doesn't always look like hair. The horns of a rhinoceros are actually made of very tightly packed hair. The spines of a hedgehog are special hairs as well.

KEEPING WARM

An animal's body needs to be at the right temperature to work properly. Mammals can keep their bodies at a fairly constant temperature, whatever the weather. Because of this, mammals can be active even in extremely cold conditions. Birds are the only other animals that can do this.

Reptiles, such as snakes and lizards, have to sit in the sun to get warm and move into the shade to cool down. Unlike mammals, they become very slow-moving when it is cold.

Mammals control their temperature by generating heat inside their bodies. They get this heat from the food they eat. This means that mammals have to eat more than most other animals. Some parts of the body, such as the muscles, make more heat than other parts. The warmth is spread evenly through the body by the blood, which is moved through a network of **blood vessels** by the mammal's **heart**.

▶ Because mammals can generate their own heat they can stay active in cold conditions. This bobcat is active enough to chase the snowshoe rabbit, which is active enough to run away!

Did you know?

The musk ox lives in the far north, where the winters are very cold. To help keep it warm it has the longest hair of any animal – growing to almost a yard long.

The heat that the mammal makes is always being lost to its surroundings. To help prevent this, most mammals have fur or hair. This traps a layer of air next to the animal's skin. Heat doesn't travel very well through the air, so this helps to keep the animal warm.

Mammals that don't have much hair save heat by reducing the flow of blood near the surface of their skin. Whales, which spend their lives in the cold oceans, have a thick layer of fat, called **blubber,** under their skin. This helps to keep the heat in.

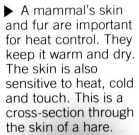

▶ A mammal's skin and fur are important for heat control. They keep it warm and dry. The skin is also sensitive to heat, cold and touch. This is a cross-section through the skin of a hare.

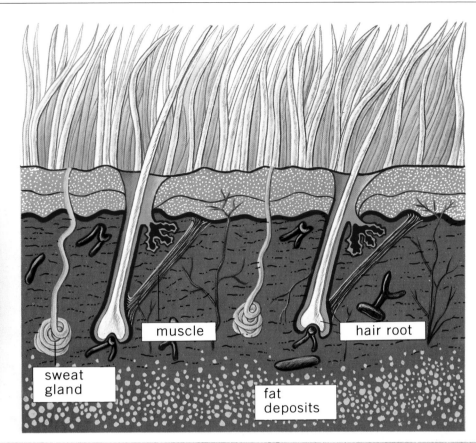

muscle

hair root

sweat gland

fat deposits

KEEPING COOL

Mammals have a variety of ways of keeping warm, but sometimes they need to cool down. A mammal that makes its own heat might become over-heated on a hot day or if it has been running fast or working hard.

One way to cool down is to increase the flow of warm blood near the surface of the skin, particularly where the hair is thin. The heat in the blood can then escape more easily. This is the opposite of what happens when the mammal is trying to save heat.

Another way that heat can be lost is through **evaporation**. When water changes from a liquid to a gas it uses up a lot of heat energy. Some mammals have special **sweat glands** in their skin. These produce a liquid that covers the skin when the mammal is hot. As this liquid, which is mostly water, evaporates, it cools the mammal.

Mammals that don't sweat a lot must cool themselves in other ways. Some will lick themselves all over so that their saliva does the same job as sweat. Elephants and some other mammals cover themselves with mud. As the mud dries out it helps cool them, as well as protecting them from insects and the sun. Some mammals, such as dogs, cool themselves by panting. By doing this they lose some of the moisture from their **lungs**, cooling their bodies from the inside.

Keeping cool is particularly important for mammals that live where it is very hot and dry — in the desert, for example.

▼ To stay cool on a hot day, elephants often spray themselves and one another with water. These are African elephants.

◀ Members of the dog family, such as this coyote, cool down by panting when they get too hot.

▼ The desert-living fennec fox hides in a burrow during the hottest part of the day. Its big ears also help it keep cool, as heat from the blood can escape more easily where there is little or no fur to stop it.

Many live in burrows and emerge only during the cold desert night. Camels, however, can store heat in the daytime by letting their bodies warm up. They cool down again at night. They do not sweat or pant because it is hard to replace the water lost.

▲ This warthog in Kenya has found a cool, muddy pool in which to wallow and escape from the heat.

MOTHERS AND BABIES

Mammals are different from all other animals in the way they look after their young. It is most often the female that does this because female mammals are unique in the animal world. Nearly all animals have to catch or gather a supply of food to give to their young, but female mammals can make their own.

▲ This female black bear produces milk to feed her growing cubs.

The females have **mammary glands** — sometimes called breasts or udders — which produce milk. The number of mammary glands varies depending on how many young the mammal usually has. Milk contains fat, protein, sugar, vitamins, salts and water – all the food a very young animal needs. The young mammal feeds on the milk by sucking on a nipple or teat.

▶ Humans are also mammals. This baby gets milk from its mother's breast.

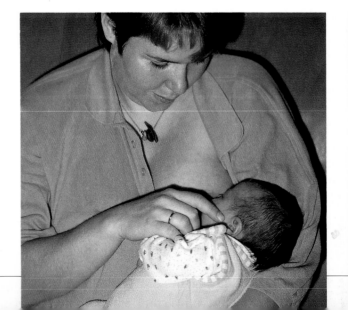

The duck-billed platypus is an unusual mammal because it lays eggs. When the eggs hatch, the young are still very small and helpless.

Almost all mammals give birth to live young. But there are three kinds that are very unusual – the duck-billed platypus and two types of spiny anteater. These mammals lay eggs, which hatch after about ten days. The duck-billed platypus lays its eggs in a nest, but the spiny anteater has a special pouch on its body to hold its egg. The egg-laying mammals do not have nipples. Their milk is a thick substance that is secreted from the skin and licked by the young.

Some young mammals make a difficult journey to reach the nipples. These mammals are called **marsupials** and include kangaroos, opossums and koalas. The young are born blind and very small – a newborn kangaroo weighs less than one-third of an ounce. The tiny animal must crawl up its mother's body using only its front legs to find a nipple. Once it reaches one, it remains attached for up to two months. Many marsupials have a pouch to protect their slowly growing young.

◀ ▲ When these young opossums (left) were first born they were naked, blind and practically helpless. They fastened on to the teats (above) in their mother's pouch while they grew.

GROWING UP

Some young mammals have to be able to move on their own from a very early age. Within a few hours of being born, most young hoofed mammals can stand up and run after their mothers. This is very important, because if they were to be left behind, they would soon be attacked by **predators**. Hoofed mammals usually have very long legs in comparison to the rest of their bodies when they are born.

All young mammals are looked after by one or both parents. Sometimes a group of animals will share the responsibility of looking after the young. Female African elephants may live together as a small group of two or three adults with their young. Hunting dogs live together in packs, and all the adults, not just the parents, will bring food back to the den for the pups.

▲ A young wildebeest is able to stand up and follow its mother almost as soon as it is born.

▼ After a successful hunt, an adult hunting dog brings food back to the den for its pups carried in its stomach.

Young whales, which are born in the water, have to be helped to the surface by their mothers or other females to take their first breath of air, since they, like all other mammals, are air-breathing animals.

One of the things that makes mammals different from other animals is their **intelligence** – mammals are the smartest animals. For many young mammals, part of growing up involves learning how to survive, often by copying the adults. Some mammals have to learn hunting skills. Adult cats, for instance, will bring small animals for their kittens to practice catching.

Some mammals that spend a lot of time swimming have to learn how to do it. Female otters often have to push their unwilling young into the water.

Human children have to spend an especially long time learning to be adults. Probably this is because their lives are so complicated.

▼ This adult meerkat has been left to babysit while the other adults of its group are away on a hunt.

▼ The female sloth carries her baby with her as she moves through the rain forest trees.

WALKING AND RUNNING

▶ The capybara of South America usually walks on its toes but can rest by putting the soles of its feet on the ground.

Almost all mammals move around on four legs. When they walk, they move one leg at a time, always keeping at least three legs on the ground. But when a mammal starts to run, its legs move very quickly, and for a moment all four legs can be off the ground at once.

▼ The hooves of the klipspringer, a type of antelope from Africa, give it a good grip on rocky surfaces.

Not all mammals put their feet on the ground in the same way. Some, such as bears and shrews, put the whole underside of each foot on the ground. These mammals often have thick skin on the soles of their feet to protect them. Many types of mammal walk on their toes. The heels of dogs and cats never touch the ground. What you might think of as a dog's knee is actually its ankle. Thick pads behind the claws on the tips of the toes give

protection and extra grip.

The longest-legged mammals are the swift-running mammals, such as deer and horses. These mammals have long foot bones and walk on the very tips of their toes. The tip of each set of toes is protected by a tough **hoof**. Hooves, claws and nails are all made of keratin, the same substance that is found in hair.

Some mammals can run very fast. Cheetahs reach more than 70 mph, and some antelopes are only a little slower.

▲ Some mammals, such as this pygmy shrew, walk on the soles of their feet.

▼ The long-legged cheetah is built for speed. It can sprint at more than 70 mph.

JUMPING, SWIMMING AND FLYING

There are some mammals that don't move around on four legs. Humans are the most obvious example. Kangaroos also move around on two legs. They hop along by pushing off the ground with their very large feet and powerful back legs.

Some mammals spend much of their time in the water. Seals and walruses come onto land only occasionally. In water, seals use their legs, called flippers, which are like broad paddles, to propel themselves along. Some seals use both their front and back flippers; others use only the back ones. Because they are so suited to swimming these animals find it difficult to move when they are on land.

▲ Using the powerful muscles of their back legs, kangaroos are able to bound 20 feet in one leap.

◄ The leopard seal is a fast-swimming hunter. This one has caught a penguin chick.

Whales and dolphins never come onto land at all. They swim by moving their tails up and down, in contrast to fish, which move their tails from side to side.

Many mammals are suited to a life in the trees. Squirrels have sharp claws to help them cling on when they climb and long back legs to help them jump from branch to branch. Flying squirrels have a large flap of skin between each front and back leg. By holding these flaps open they can glide from tree to tree, steering themselves with their tails.

▲ Jumping from high branches, the flying squirrel can glide for more than 1300 feet.

One type of mammal really can fly. Bats have very long, thin fingers, with skin stretched between them. This skin is also attached to the bat's ankles, forming the bat's wings. Some bats are no bigger than bumblebees. Others have a wingspan of almost five feet.

▶ Bats are the only mammals that have wings and really can fly. This leaf-nosed bat is about to grab an insect to eat.

Did you know?

Some whales can dive to depths of more than half a mile.

Sometimes a whale will stay underwater for two hours, but it has to come up to the surface to breathe eventually.

TEETH AND JAWS

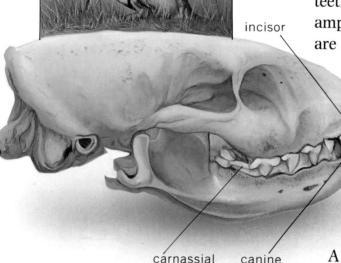

incisor

carnassial   canine

▲ The teeth of a cat, such as a lion, are suited to eating meat.

Many different types of animals have teeth. Fish have teeth, and so do amphibians and reptiles. Mammals' teeth are different from those of other animals, however. For instance, mammals are the only animals to have two sets of teeth. They have one set, sometimes called **milk teeth**, when they are young, and another set, called permanent or adult teeth, that grow when they are older.

A lot of other animals have teeth that are all alike. Many use them only to grip their food. A mammal's teeth are not all the same. The sort of teeth it has depends on the sort of food it eats. Bears, dogs, weasels and other animals that eat meat have teeth that are suited to that job. At the front of the mouth are sharp, bladelike teeth called **incisors** that are used to scrape meat from bones. Next to these are the large, pointed **canine** teeth. These can help to hold and kill other animals. At the back of the mouth are the **carnassial** teeth. The top and bottom sets come together like shears to cut away flesh and crunch bones. The jaws of meat-eating mammals move up and down.

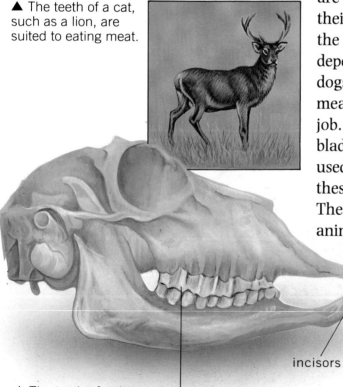

incisors

▲ The teeth of a deer are suited to a diet of plants.

cheek teeth

Cattle, horses, deer and other mammals that eat plants have different types of teeth. They only have incisors in the front of the lower jaw. These bite against a strong pad in the upper jaw and are used to cut through grass or other plants. There is a big gap between front and back teeth. The back, or cheek, teeth have flat tops and are close together to make a large surface for grinding tough plant material.

The jaws of plant-eating mammals move from side to side to grind the teeth together. This grinding movement wears away the teeth, which grow throughout the animal's life to make up for this. The incisors of **rodents**, such as rats and beavers, who gnaw away at their food, also grow throughout their lives.

Mammals that have a varied diet, such as humans and chimpanzees, have teeth that are somewhere in between those of meat eaters and plant eaters. Their jaws can move up and down and from side to side.

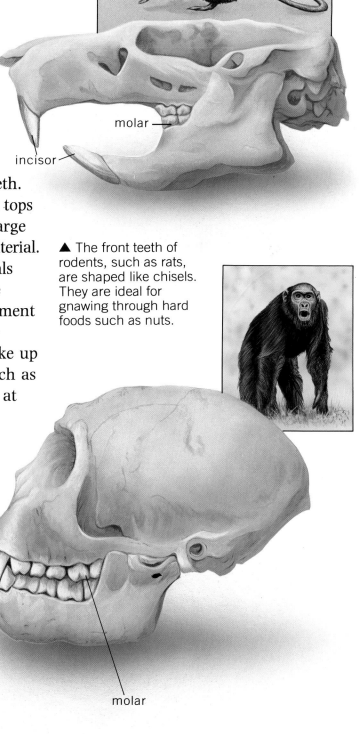

molar

incisor

▲ The front teeth of rodents, such as rats, are shaped like chisels. They are ideal for gnawing through hard foods such as nuts.

incisor

canine

molar

▶ The teeth of apes, such as chimpanzees, allow them to eat a mixed diet of both plants and meat.

SCENT AND TASTE

▲ The long nose and long, sticky tongue of the spiny anteater are used to find and catch the insects it eats.

Many types of mammal are most active either at night or at sunrise or sunset. For these animals, smelling and hearing

what is going on around them are more important than seeing it. How mammals hear is discussed on pages 24 and 25.

Insects detect smells using the **antennae** on their heads, but most animals have cavities in their heads where their scent detectors are located. In mammals, scent detectors are found inside the upper part of the nose.

Some mammals, such as cats and mice, have an extra scent detector in the roof of the mouth. It is particularly sensitive to the smell of animals of the opposite sex and helps them find a **mate**. Some reptiles have extra scent detectors too.

◀ Rats, like many mammals, use their sense of taste to learn to avoid eating foods that have made them ill before.

Most mammals have special glands for making some sort of scent, which they use to announce to other mammals where their **territory** is. Some, such as the hippopotamus, will spray dung around, and cats, such as lions, will use urine.

The difference between smelling and tasting is that things can be smelled at a distance but have to be touched to be tasted. The part of the body mammals use for tasting is the tongue. This is where the **taste buds** are found. The sense of taste helps the animal to decide if something will be good to eat. For example, rats learn to avoid eating food that has a certain taste if they have been made ill by it before.

▶ This male lion is marking out his territory. The smell of his urine will warn other lions that he is nearby.

THE MAMMAL EAR

▶ The ears of all mammals contain three tiny bones to pick up sound vibrations. Amphibians, reptiles and birds have only a single bone.

▼ The marsh deer of Brazil is always listening for danger. Its large ears are pricked, alert for any sound.

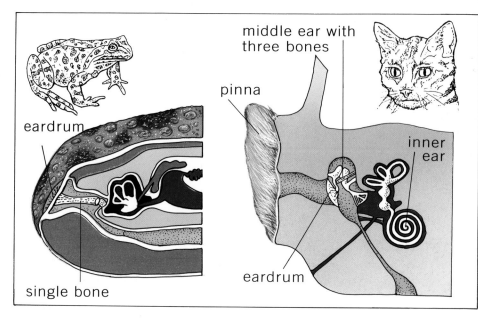

eardrum

single bone

middle ear with three bones

pinna

inner ear

eardrum

Many mammals have sensitive ears that can pick up very faint sounds. The flaps of skin on the sides of your head that you probably call your ears are just the outer parts. Most mammals have these outer ears. They are the only animals that have them.

The outer ear, or **pinna**, helps to collect and concentrate sounds. Many mammals can move their pinnae around into the best position to pick up sound. Try putting your hands behind your ears to make the collecting area bigger. Can you hear a difference?

Inside, a mammal's ear is different from that of all other animals. All mammals have three tiny bones inside each ear that pass the sound vibrations along to where they are heard. Amphibians, reptiles and birds have only a single bone.

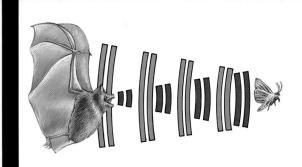

For two types of mammal, hearing is especially important. Most bats spend much of their time flying around in the dark. How do they know where they are going? The answer is that they use sound. The bat lets out a very high-pitched click or call, often too high for human ears to hear. It then listens for the **echo** of its call. From the way the sound bounces back to its ears the bat can tell what is around it. Some bats have huge ears to pick up the sounds.

Whales and dolphins face a similar problem when they are swimming in murky water or at night, and they have a similar solution. Like bats, these mammals make high-pitched sounds and can detect what is in the water by listening for the echo.

The diagram (top) shows how sound bounces off an object to create an echo. A bat, such as this horseshoe bat, squeaks as it hunts, and its sensitive ears can pick up the echo of its call bouncing back from an insect. This enables a bat to hunt insects in the dark by *hearing* where they are.

THE MAMMAL EYE

A mammal's eyes can tell you something about the sort of life it lives. For instance, mammals such as deer and rabbits, which are hunted by other mammals, need to be constantly on the lookout. Their eyes are on the sides of the head so that they can see as much as possible all at once.

In contrast, mammals that are hunters have eyes on the front of the head. This means that they see two slightly different images of the same thing. The animal's brain combines the two images so that it doesn't see double. The slight difference allows the animal to judge distance. This is called **binocular vision**.

▶ The tiger's front-facing eyes help it to hunt down other animals.

26

A hunter such as a cat knows how far to jump to land on a mouse. Monkeys, squirrels and other tree-living mammals also have binocular vision, enabling them to judge the distance between tree branches. Humans can judge how to catch a ball.

Many insects must see in color to help them find flowers. Birds, reptiles and fish are thought to have color vision because of the way they respond to different colors.

People argue about whether or not mammals see in color. We know that we do, and we are mammals, but what about the others? Some people think that only humans and other apes have color vision. Others think that probably all mammals have some sort of color vision, but that some mammals might be better than others at seeing certain colors.

The problem is that so much of seeing goes on in the brain, where signals from the eyes are turned into pictures. Since we cannot be a giraffe or a rat or a fox, we cannot really know what sort of picture its brain is making.

The tarsiers of Southeast Asia are active at night. Their huge eyes let them see in the darkness.

FELLOW MAMMALS

Although mammals have been around since the time of the dinosaurs, they didn't really begin to flourish until after the giant reptiles disappeared 65 million years ago. Today there are more than 5000 different kinds of mammal. They range in size from shrews that are smaller than hummingbirds to the giant blue whale, which is bigger than any dinosaur.

Mammals are found in some of the coldest and hottest places on Earth.

There are mammals that fly and mammals that spend their lives in water.

All mammals have some hair, and many are completely covered with fur. They have specialized teeth to deal with their food. They also have three bones in their ear, unlike other animals. Female mammals produce milk to feed their young.

Mammals also have a high degree of intelligence. Many live in organized societies and communicate with one another through a language of sounds and body postures. Young mammals learn much of what they need to know from their parents. They also spend a lot of time playing. Sound familiar?

Mammals such as whales, dolphins, wolves, chimpanzees, and gorillas are among the most intelligent animals on Earth. We like to think that we are the smartest of all. No other creature can match our ability to change the world around us. But we are changing it so much these days that other animals may not be able to survive much longer. Perhaps we will learn to use our intelligence instead to protect our fellow mammals and all of nature to keep this world a wondrous place.

Dolphins are intelligent, ocean-living mammals. They communicate with one another using a range of squeaks and calls.

GLOSSARY

Antennae: The feelers on an insect's head that it uses for touching, smelling and tasting.

Binocular vision: Seeing something with both eyes at the same time; this allows an animal to judge distance.

Blood vessels: The network of tubes, called veins and arteries, that carry blood around inside the body.

Blubber: The thick fat in the bodies of whales and other sea mammals that helps to keep them warm.

Canine: A sharp, pointed tooth used for killing and holding food; most meat-eating mammals have four of these teeth.

Carnassial: One of the large cutting teeth found at the back of the mouth of meat-eating mammals.

Dinosaur: The name given to reptiles that lived on Earth more than 65 million years ago; some were only a couple of feet long, but others were more than 80 feet and weighed 100 tons.

Echo: A sound that has bounced back from something so that it can be heard again.

Evaporation: This is what happens when liquid water turns into the gas called water vapor without boiling.

Heart: The part of the body that pumps the blood through the blood vessels.

Hoof: A hard covering of keratin that protects the feet of some types of mammal, such as horses and rhinoceroses.

Incisor: One of the front cutting teeth in a mammal's mouth.

Intelligence: The ability to understand and solve problems.

Keratin: A strong but flexible material that is found in hair, horns, nails and hooves.

Lungs: The parts of the body that many types of animal, including mammals, use for breathing.

Mammary glands: The parts of an adult female mammal's body that produce milk to feed her young.

Marsupial: A type of mammal whose young are very small and helpless when born; they are often protected in a special pouch in the mother's body. Kangaroos, koalas, wombats and opossums are all types of marsupial.

Mate: One of a pair of animals — one male and the other female — that will produce young together.

Milk teeth: The first set of teeth that a mammal has when it is young; these are replaced by adult teeth as the mammal gets older. Only mammals have milk teeth.

Pinna (plural: pinnae): The outer ear of a mammal that helps to collect and concentrate sound.

Predator: An animal that catches and kills other animals for food.

Rodent: A type of mammal with chisel-shaped incisors used for gnawing. There are more types of rodent than there are any other type of mammal. Rats, mice, beavers and porcupines are all types of rodent.

Sebum: An oily, waxy substance that protects and waterproofs the hair and skin of mammals.

Sweat glands: The parts just beneath the surface of the skin of some mammals that produce sweat; sweat helps to cool the body by evaporation.

Taste buds: Tiny parts of the tongue that send signals to the brain about the way something tastes.

Territory: The area in which an animal lives and that it will defend against others. Many mammals use their own scents to mark their territories.

Vibrissae: Another name for whiskers, the long, stiff hairs around the nose of many mammals. They are used for touch.

INDEX